C000148381

Cram101 Textbook Outlines to accompany:

Strategize! : Experiential Exercises in Strategic Management

C. Gopinath; Julie I. Siciliano, 3rd Edition

A Content Technologies Inc. publication (c) 2012.

STUDYING MADE EASY

This Cram101 notebook is designed to make studying easier and increase your comprehension of the textbook material. Instead of starting with a blank notebook and trying to write down everything discussed in class lectures, you can use this Cram101 textbook notebook and annotate your notes along with the lecture.

Our goal is to give you the best tools for success.

For a supreme understanding of the course, pair your notebook with our online tools. Should you decide you prefer Cram101.com as your study tool,

we'd like to offer you a trade...

Our Trade In program is a simple way for us to keep our promise and provide you the best studying tools, regardless of where you purchased your Cram101 textbook notebook. As long as your notebook is in *Like New Condition**, you can send it back to us and we will immediately give you a Cram101.com account free for 120 days!

Let The *Trade In* Begin!

THREE SIMPLE STEPS TO TRADE:

1. Go to www.cram101.com/tradein and fill out the packing slip information.

2. Submit and print the packing slip and mail it in with your Cram101 textbook notebook.

3. Activate your account after you receive your email confirmation.

* Books must be returned in *Like New Condition*, meaning there is no damage to the book including, but not limited to; ripped or torn pages, markings or writing on pages, or folded / creased pages. Upon receiving the book, Cram101 will inspect it and reserves the right to terminate your free Cram101.com account and return your textbook notebook at the owners expense.

Learning System

Cram101 Textbook Outlines is a learning system. The notes in this book are the highlights of your textbook, you will never have to highlight a book again.

How to use this book. Take this book to class, it is your notebook for the lecture. The notes and highlights on the left hand side of the pages follow the outline and order of the textbook. All you have to do is follow along while your instructor presents the lecture. Circle the items emphasized in class and add other important information on the right side. With Cram101 Textbook Outlines you'll spend less time writing and more time listening. Learning becomes more efficient.

Cram101.com Online

Increase your studying efficiency by using Cram101.com's practice tests and online reference material. It is the perfect complement to Cram101 Textbook Outlines. Use self-teaching matching tests or simulate in-class testing with comprehensive multiple choice tests, or simply use Cram's true and false tests for quick review. Cram101.com even allows you to enter your in-class notes for an integrated studying format combining the textbook notes with your class notes.

Visit **www.Cram101.com**, click Sign Up at the top of the screen, and enter **DK73DW14351** in the promo code box on the registration screen. Your access to www.Cram101.com is discounted by 50% because you have purchased this book. Sign up and stop highlighting textbooks forever.

Strategize! : Experiential Exercises in Strategic Management
C. Gopinath; Julie I. Siciliano, 3rd

CONTENTS

Chapter 1. UNDERSTANDING STRATEGIC MANAGEMENT

Decision making	Decision making can be regarded as the mental processes (cognitive process) resulting in the selection of a course of action among several alternative scenarios. Every decision making process produces a final choice. The output can be an action or an opinion of choice.
Perspective	Perspective in the graphic arts, such as drawing, is an approximate representation, on a flat surface (such as paper), of an image as it is seen by the eye. The two most characteristic features of perspective are that objects are drawn: • Smaller as their distance from the observer increases • Foreshortened: the size of an object's dimensions along the line of sight are relatively shorter than dimensions across the line of sight Overview Linear perspective works by representing the light that passes from a scene through an imaginary rectangle (the painting), to the viewer's eye. It is similar to a viewer looking through a window and painting what is seen directly onto the windowpane.
Competitive advantage	Competitive advantage is defined as the strategic advantage one business entity has over its rival entities within its competitive industry. Achieving competitive advantage strengthens and positions a business better within the business environment. Resource-based view perspective Competitive advantage is a theory that seeks to address some of the criticisms of comparative advantage.

Chapter 1. UNDERSTANDING STRATEGIC MANAGEMENT

Exercise	The owner of an option contract may exercise it, indicating that the financial transaction specified by the contract is to be enacted immediately between the two parties, and the contract itself is terminated. When exercising a call, the owner of the option purchases the underlying shares at the strike price from the option seller, while for a put, the owner of the option sells the underlying to the option seller. Exercise Type The option style determines when, how, and under what circumstances, the option holder may exercise.
Position	In financial trading, a position is a binding commitment to buy or sell a given amount of financial instruments, such as securities, currencies or commodities, for a given price. The term "position" is also used in the context of finance for the amount of securities or commodities held by a person, firm, or institution, and for the ownership status of a person's or institution's investments. Trading and financial assets In derivatives trading or for financial instruments, the concept of a position is used heavily.
Strategy	Strategy, a word of military origin, refers to a plan of action designed to achieve a particular goal. In military usage strategy is distinct from tactics, which are concerned with the conduct of an engagement, while strategy is concerned with how different engagements are linked. How a battle is fought is a matter of tactics: the terms and conditions that it is fought on and whether it should be fought at all is a matter of strategy, which is part of the four levels of warfare: political goals or grand strategy, strategy, operations, and tactics.
Core	A core is a device used in casting and molding processes to produce internal cavities and reentrant angles. The core is normally a disposable item that is destroyed to get it out of the piece. They are most commonly used in sand casting, but are also used in injection molding.

Chapter 1. UNDERSTANDING STRATEGIC MANAGEMENT

Mission statement	A mission statement is a formal, short, written statement of the purpose of a company or organization. The mission statement should guide the actions of the organization, spell out its overall goal, provide a sense of direction, and guide decision-making. It provides "the framework or context within which the company's strategies are formulated." Historically it is associated with Christian religious groups; indeed, for many years, a missionary was assumed to be a person on a specifically religious mission.
Course	A course is a continuous horizontal layer of similarly-sized building material one unit high, usually in a wall. The term is almost always used in conjunction with unit masonry such as brick, cut stone, or concrete masonry units ("concrete block").
	Styles
	Stretcher - The typical course style, masonry units are laid with their face parallel to the wall and the long dimension outwards.
	Header - a course with the face of the unit parallel to the wall, and the small dimension outwards, often used to interlock two adjacent wythes.
	Rowlock - A course with the long dimension parallel to the wall and the small face looking outward.
Airlines	Airlines is an MS-DOS based construction and management simulation game created by Interactivision later renamed InterActive Vision. The main object of the game was to successfully set up an airline by buying aircraft, planning routes, setting ticket prices and dealing with events such as hostage and oil crises. The game had 4 airlines, a minimum of one of which was human controlled, the rest computer controlled.
Sample	In general, a sample is a limited quantity of something which is intended to be similar to and represent a larger amount of that thing(s).
Team	TEAM, formerly known as Team of Destiny, is a leadership development company founded by Orrin Woodward and Chris Brady in 1999 in Michigan. TEAM is an acronym that stands for TEAM.

Woodward and Brady are former IBOs (Independent Business Owners, a.k.a. distributors) of the multi-level marketing company Quixtar, as well as members of the board of directors of Quixtar's IBOAI (IBO Association International, representing Quixtar IBOs).

Chief executive	Chief Executive is a term used for certain gubernatorial offices, expressing the nature of their job being analogous to a head of government. Commonly used to refer to Presidential powers given by the constitution. As Chief Executive the president can: implement policy, supervise executive branch of government, prepare executive budget for submission to congress, and appoint and remove executive officials

While in most cases there is another specific style, such as (lieutenant-)governor(-general), there are a few offices formally styled Chief Executive:

- in the People's Republic of China, in two special administrative regions that were under foreign colonial rule until their recent transfer of sovereignty, where the chief executive are heads of the regions and heads of government:

- in Mauritius, on Rodrigues island, since 12 October 2002 autonomy was granted:

- New Zealand Antarctic Territory: while not a government, the Ross Dependency is a Crown entity managed by a Board of Directors and the Chair acts as the Chief Executive.

Chief executive officer	A chief executive officer, managing director, or chief executive is the highest-ranking corporate officer (executive) or administrator in charge of total management of an organization. An individual appointed as a Chief executive officer of a corporation, company, organization, or agency reports to the board of directors.

Many Chief executive officers have the title "president and Chief executive officer".

Chapter 1. UNDERSTANDING STRATEGIC MANAGEMENT

Corporate governance	Corporate governance is the set of processes, customs, policies, laws, and institutions affecting the way a corporation (or company) is directed, administered or controlled. Corporate governance also includes the relationships among the many stakeholders involved and the goals for which the corporation is governed. The principal stakeholders are the shareholders, the board of directors, executives, employees, customers, creditors, suppliers, and the community at large.
Institutional theory	Institutional theory is "A widely accepted theoretical posture that emphasizes rational myths, isomorphism, and legitimacy." F There are two dominant trends in institutional theory: • Old Institutionalism sometimes associated with Historical institutionalism • New institutionalism Institutional theory focuses on the deeper and more resilient aspects of social structure. It considers the processes by which structures, including schemas, rules, norms, and routines, become established as authoritative guidelines for social behavior. Different components of institutional theory explain how these elements are created, diffused, adopted, and adapted over space and time; and how they fall into decline and disuse.
Board of directors	A board of directors is a body of elected or appointed members who jointly oversee the activities of a company or organization. The body sometimes has a different name, such as board of trustees, board of governors, board of managers, or executive board. It is often simply referred to as "the board." A board's activities are determined by the powers, duties, and responsibilities delegated to it or conferred on it by an authority outside itself.
Director	Director refers to a rank in management. A director is a person who leads, or supervises a certain area of a company, a program, or a project. Usually companies, which use this title commonly have large numbers of people with the title of director with different categories (e.g. director of human resources).

Chapter 1. UNDERSTANDING STRATEGIC MANAGEMENT

Corporation	A corporation is a legal entity that is created under the laws of a State designed to establish the entity as a separate legal entity having its own privileges and liabilities distinct from those of its members. There are many different forms of corporations, most of which are used to conduct business. Early corporations were established by charter and many of these chartered companies still exist.
Enron	Enron Corporation (former NYSE ticker symbol ENE) was an American energy, commodities, and services company based in Houston, Texas. Before its bankruptcy in late 2001, Enron employed approximately 22,000 staff and was one of the world's leading electricity, natural gas, communications, and pulp and paper companies, with claimed revenues of nearly $101 billion in 2000. Fortune named Enron "America's Most Innovative Company" for six consecutive years. At the end of 2001, it was revealed that its reported financial condition was sustained substantially by institutionalized, systematic, and creatively planned accounting fraud, known as the "Enron scandal".
Line	The notion of line or straight line was introduced by the ancient mathematicians to represent straight objects with negligible width and depth. Lines are an idealization of such objects. Thus, until seventeenth century, lines were defined like this: "The line is the first species of quantity, which has only one dimension, namely length, without any width nor depth, and is nothing else than the flow or run of the point which [...] will leave from its imaginary moving some vestige in length, exempt of any width.
John Smedley	John Smedley is the name of four generations of owners of Lea Mills, near Matlock, Derbyshire. The most famous of these was John Smedley born Wirksworth, Derbyshire. Lea Mills Lea Mills was founded in 1784 by Peter Nightingale (an ancestor of Florence Nightingale) (former accountant to Richard Arkwright), and John Smedley.
Frank	FRANK is the United Kingdom government's national anti-drug campaign. The campaign was established in 2003 and is principally aimed at teenagers. It is advertised and promoted through TV, radio, and the web.

Chapter 1. UNDERSTANDING STRATEGIC MANAGEMENT

Community	Community is a British trade union representing workers in the iron and steel, clothing, textiles, footwear and betting industries as well as workers in voluntary organisations, workshops for visually impaired and disabled people, Community Care providers and Housing Associations. Community has merged or transferred engagements with a number of smaller unions, some of which have retained their structure as sectors within Community. These include the National League of the Blind and Disabled (NLBD), the National Union of Domestic Appliance and General Operatives (NUDAGO), the Knitwear, Footwear and Apparel Trades (KFAT) and the British Union of Social Work Employees (BUSWE).
Creditor	A creditor is a party (e.g. person, organization, company, or government) that has a claim to the services of a second party. It is a person or institution to whom money is owed. The first party, in general, has provided some property or service to the second party under the assumption (usually enforced by contract) that the second party will return an equivalent property or service.
Customer	A customer is usually used to refer to a current or potential buyer or user of the products of an individual or organization, called the supplier, seller, or vendor. This is typically through purchasing or renting goods or services. However, in certain contexts, the term customer also includes by extension any entity that uses or experiences the services of another.
Stakeholder	A corporate stakeholder is a party that can affect or be affected by the actions of the business as a whole. The stakeholder concept was first used in a 1963 internal memorandum at the Stanford Research institute. It defined stakeholders as "those groups without whose support the organization would cease to exist." The theory was later developed and championed by R. Edward Freeman in the 1980s.
Stockholder	A mutual shareholder or Stockholder is an individual or company (including a corporation) that legally owns one or more shares of stock in a joint stock company. A company's shareholders collectively own that company. Thus, the typical goal of such companies is to enhance shareholder value.
Vendor	A vendor, is a supply chain management term meaning anyone who provides goods or services to a company. A vendor often manufactures inventoriable items, and sells those items to a customer.
	History
	The term vendor originally represented property vendors.

Clam101

Chapter 1. UNDERSTANDING STRATEGIC MANAGEMENT

Bargaining	Bargaining is a type of negotiation in which the buyer and seller of a good or service dispute the price which will be paid and the exact nature of the transaction that will take place, and eventually come to an agreement. Bargaining is an alternative pricing strategy to fixed prices. Optimally, if it costs the retailer nothing to engage and allow bargaining, he can divine the buyer's willingness to spend.
Bargaining power	Bargaining power is a concept related to the relative abilities of parties in a situation to exert influence over each other. If both parties are on an equal footing in a debate, then they will have equal bargaining power, such as in a perfectly competitive market, or between an evenly matched monopoly and monopsony.
	There are a number of fields where the concept of bargaining power has proven crucial to coherent analysis: game theory, labour economics, collective bargaining arrangements, diplomatic negotiations, settlement of litigation, the price of insurance, and any negotiation in general.
Bear Stearns	The Bear Stearns Companies, Inc. (former NYSE ticker symbol BSC) based in New York City, was a global investment bank and securities trading and brokerage, until its collapse and fire sale to JPMorgan Chase in 2008. The main business areas, based on 2006 net revenue distributions, were capital markets (equities, fixed income, investment banking; just under 80%), wealth management (under 10%), and global clearing services (12%).
	Bear Stearns was involved in securitization and issued huge amounts of asset-backed securities, which in the case of mortgages were pioneered by Lewis S. Ranieri, "the father of mortgage securities".
Federal Reserve	The Federal Reserve System is the central banking system of the United States. It was created in 1913 by the enactment of the Federal Reserve Act, largely as a response to a series of financial panics or bank runs, particularly a severe panic in 1907. Over time, the roles and responsibilities of the Federal Reserve System have expanded and its structure has evolved. Events such as the Great Depression were some of the major factors leading to changes in the system. Its duties today, according to official Federal Reserve documentation, fall into four general areas:

· Conducting the nation's monetary policy by influencing the monetary and credit conditions in the economy in pursuit of maximum employment, stable prices, and moderate long-term interest rates.

· Supervising and regulating banking institutions to ensure the safety and soundness of the nation's banking and financial system and to protect the credit rights of consumers.

· Maintaining the stability of the financial system and containing systemic risk that may arise in financial markets.

· Providing financial services to depository institutions, the U.S. government, and foreign official institutions, including playing a major role in operating the nation's payments system.

Loan	A loan is a type of debt. Like all debt instruments, a loan entails the redistribution of financial assets over time, between the lender and the borrower. In a loan, the borrower initially receives or borrows an amount of money, called the principal, from the lender, and is obligated to pay back or repay an equal amount of money to the lender at a later time.
Group	In mathematics, a group is an algebraic structure consisting of a set together with an operation that combines any two of its elements to form a third element. To qualify as a group, the set and the operation must satisfy a few conditions called group axioms, namely closure, associativity, identity and invertibility. Many familiar mathematical structures such as number systems obey these axioms: for example, the integers endowed with the addition operation form a group.

CRAM101

Chapter 2. DESIGNING STRATEGY

Bargaining	Bargaining is a type of negotiation in which the buyer and seller of a good or service dispute the price which will be paid and the exact nature of the transaction that will take place, and eventually come to an agreement. Bargaining is an alternative pricing strategy to fixed prices. Optimally, if it costs the retailer nothing to engage and allow bargaining, he can divine the buyer's willingness to spend.
Bargaining power	Bargaining power is a concept related to the relative abilities of parties in a situation to exert influence over each other. If both parties are on an equal footing in a debate, then they will have equal bargaining power, such as in a perfectly competitive market, or between an evenly matched monopoly and monopsony. There are a number of fields where the concept of bargaining power has proven crucial to coherent analysis: game theory, labour economics, collective bargaining arrangements, diplomatic negotiations, settlement of litigation, the price of insurance, and any negotiation in general.
Obstacle	An obstacle, is an object, thing, action or situation that causes an obstruction, forms a barrier, creates a difficulty, a nuisance or a disorder to achieve concrete goals. There are, therefore, different types of obstacles, which can be physical, economic, biopsychosocial, cultural, political, technological or even military. Physical barriers As physical obstacles, we can enumerate all those physical barriers that block the action and prevent the progress or the achievement of a concrete goal.
Barriers to entry	In theories of competition in economics, barriers to entry are obstacles that make it difficult to enter a given market. The term can refer to hindrances a firm faces in trying to enter a market or industry - such as government regulation, or a large, established firm taking advantage of economies of scale - or those an individual faces in trying to gain entrance to a profession - such as education or licensing requirements.

Chapter 2. DESIGNING STRATEGY

	Because barriers to entry protect incumbent firms and restrict competition in a market, they can contribute to distortionary prices.
Entry	In economics, entry into a market means becoming a supplier of goods or services. Monopolies have an incentive to create barriers to entry.
Vendor	A vendor, is a supply chain management term meaning anyone who provides goods or services to a company. A vendor often manufactures inventoriable items, and sells those items to a customer. History The term vendor originally represented property vendors.
Strategy	Strategy, a word of military origin, refers to a plan of action designed to achieve a particular goal. In military usage strategy is distinct from tactics, which are concerned with the conduct of an engagement, while strategy is concerned with how different engagements are linked. How a battle is fought is a matter of tactics: the terms and conditions that it is fought on and whether it should be fought at all is a matter of strategy, which is part of the four levels of warfare: political goals or grand strategy, strategy, operations, and tactics.
Complementors	Complementors is a term used to describe businesses that directly sell a product (or products) or service (or services) that complement the product or service of another company by adding value to mutual customers; for example, Intel and Microsoft (Pentium processors and Windows), or Microsoft ' McAfee (Microsoft Windows ' McAfee anti-virus). Complementors are sometimes called "The Sixth Force" (from Porter's Five Forces model), a term which was coined by Adam Brandenburger.

Chapter 2. DESIGNING STRATEGY

	Before its use in business, the word was used to describe a color that is complementory to another color.
Product	The noun product is defined as a "thing produced by labor or effort" or the "result of an act or a process", and stems from the verb produce, from the Latin produce(re) '(to) lead or bring forth'. Since 1575, the word "product" has referred to anything produced. Since 1695, the word has referred to "thing or things produced".
Stakeholder	A corporate stakeholder is a party that can affect or be affected by the actions of the business as a whole. The stakeholder concept was first used in a 1963 internal memorandum at the Stanford Research institute. It defined stakeholders as "those groups without whose support the organization would cease to exist." The theory was later developed and championed by R. Edward Freeman in the 1980s.
Perspective	Perspective in the graphic arts, such as drawing, is an approximate representation, on a flat surface (such as paper), of an image as it is seen by the eye. The two most characteristic features of perspective are that objects are drawn: • Smaller as their distance from the observer increases • Foreshortened: the size of an object's dimensions along the line of sight are relatively shorter than dimensions across the line of sight Overview Linear perspective works by representing the light that passes from a scene through an imaginary rectangle (the painting), to the viewer's eye. It is similar to a viewer looking through a window and painting what is seen directly onto the windowpane.
Commission	The payment of commission as remuneration for services rendered or products sold is a common way to reward sales people. Payments often will be calculated on the basis of a percentage of the goods sold. This is a way for firms to solve the principal-agent problem, by attempting to realign employees' interests with those of the firm.

Clam101

Chapter 2. DESIGNING STRATEGY

Native American Gaming	Native American gaming enterprises are gaming businesses operated on Indian reservations or tribal land in the United States. Indian tribes have limited sovereignty over these businesses and therefore are granted the ability to establish gambling enterprises outside of direct state regulation. History of native american Gaming In the very early 1970s, Russell and Helen Bryan, a married Chippewa couple living in a mobile home on Indian lands in northern Minnesota, received a property tax bill from the local county, Itasca County.
Group	In mathematics, a group is an algebraic structure consisting of a set together with an operation that combines any two of its elements to form a third element. To qualify as a group, the set and the operation must satisfy a few conditions called group axioms, namely closure, associativity, identity and invertibility. Many familiar mathematical structures such as number systems obey these axioms: for example, the integers endowed with the addition operation form a group.
SWOT analysis	SWOT analysis is a strategic planning method used to evaluate the Strengths, Weaknesses, Opportunities, and Threats involved in a project or in a business venture. It involves specifying the objective of the business venture or project and identifying the internal and external factors that are favorable and unfavorable to achieve that objective. The technique is credited to Albert Humphrey, who led a convention at Stanford University in the 1960s and 1970s using data from Fortune 500 companies.
Matrix	In hot metal typesetting, a matrix is a mold for casting the letters known as sorts used in letterpress printing. In letterpress typography the matrix of one letter is inserted into the bottom of a hand mould, the mould is locked and molten type metal is poured into a straight-sided vertical cavity above the matrix. When the metal has cooled and solidified the mould is unlocked and a newly-cast metal sort is removed, ready for composition with other sorts.

Chapter 2. DESIGNING STRATEGY

Competitive advantage	Competitive advantage is defined as the strategic advantage one business entity has over its rival entities within its competitive industry. Achieving competitive advantage strengthens and positions a business better within the business environment. Resource-based view perspective Competitive advantage is a theory that seeks to address some of the criticisms of comparative advantage.
Cost	In business, retail, and accounting, a cost is the value of money that has been used up to produce something, and hence is not available for use anymore. In economics, a cost is an alternative that is given up as a result of a decision. In business, the cost may be one of acquisition, in which case the amount of money expended to acquire it is counted as cost.
Cost leadership	Cost leadership is a concept developed by Michael Porter, used in business strategy. It describes a way to establish the competitive advantage. Cost leadership, in basic words, means the lowest cost of operation in the industry.
Differentiation	Differentiation is a concept used in business strategy and describes one of the three ways to establish competitive advantage. Differentiation advantage occurs when a firm delivers greater services for a non-unlimited higher price than its competitors. They are collectively known as positional advantages because they denote the firm's position in its industry as a leader in either superior services or cost.
Niche market	A niche market is the subset of the market on which a specific product is focusing; therefore the market niche defines the specific product features aimed at satisfying specific market needs, as well as the price range, production quality and the demographics that is intended to impact. Every single product that is on sale can be defined by its niche market. As of special note, the products aimed at a wide demographic audience, with the resulting low price (due to price elasticity of demand), are said to belong to the mainstream niche--in practice referred to only as mainstream or of high demand. Narrower demographics lead to elevated prices due to the same principle. So to speak, the Niche Market is the highly specialized market that tries to survive among the competition from numerous super companies.

Chapter 2. DESIGNING STRATEGY

Core	A core is a device used in casting and molding processes to produce internal cavities and reentrant angles. The core is normally a disposable item that is destroyed to get it out of the piece. They are most commonly used in sand casting, but are also used in injection molding.
Position	In financial trading, a position is a binding commitment to buy or sell a given amount of financial instruments, such as securities, currencies or commodities, for a given price.
	The term "position" is also used in the context of finance for the amount of securities or commodities held by a person, firm, or institution, and for the ownership status of a person's or institution's investments.
	Trading and financial assets
	In derivatives trading or for financial instruments, the concept of a position is used heavily.
Lodging	Lodging is a type of residential accommodation. People who travel and stay away from home for more than a day need lodging for sleep, rest, safety, shelter from cold temperatures or rain, storage of luggage and access to common household functions.
	Lodgings may be self catering in which case no food is laid on but cooking facilities are available.
Team	TEAM, formerly known as Team of Destiny, is a leadership development company founded by Orrin Woodward and Chris Brady in 1999 in Michigan. TEAM is an acronym that stands for TEAM.
	Woodward and Brady are former IBOs (Independent Business Owners, a.k.a. distributors) of the multi-level marketing company Quixtar, as well as members of the board of directors of Quixtar's IBOAI (IBO Association International, representing Quixtar IBOs).

Chapter 2. DESIGNING STRATEGY

Management	Management in all business and organizational activities is the act of getting people together to accomplish desired goals and objectives using available resources efficiently and effectively. Management comprises planning, organizing, staffing, leading or directing, and controlling an organization (a group of one or more people or entities) or effort for the purpose of accomplishing a goal. Resourcing encompasses the deployment and manipulation of human resources, financial resources, technological resources, and natural resources.
Senior management	Senior management is generally a team of individuals at the highest level of organizational management who have the day-to-day responsibilities of managing a company or corporation, they hold specific executive powers conferred onto them with and by authority of the board of directors and/or the shareholders. There are most often higher levels of responsibility, such as a board of directors and those who own the company (shareholders), but they focus on managing the senior or executive management instead of the day-to-day activities of the business. In Project Management, senior management is responsible for authorizing the funding of projects.
Mission statement	A mission statement is a formal, short, written statement of the purpose of a company or organization. The mission statement should guide the actions of the organization, spell out its overall goal, provide a sense of direction, and guide decision-making. It provides "the framework or context within which the company's strategies are formulated." Historically it is associated with Christian religious groups; indeed, for many years, a missionary was assumed to be a person on a specifically religious mission.
Image	An image is an artifact, for example a two-dimensional picture, that has a similar appearance to some subject--usually a physical object or a person. Characteristics Images may be two-dimensional, such as a photograph, screen display, and as well as a three-dimensional, such as a statue or hologram. They may be captured by optical devices--such as cameras, mirrors, lenses, telescopes, microscopes, etc.
Price	In ordinary usage, price is the quantity of payment or compensation given by one party to another in return for goods or services.

Chapter 2. DESIGNING STRATEGY

In all modern economies, the overwhelming majority of prices are quoted in (and the transactions involve) units of some form of currency. Although in theory, prices could be quoted as quantities of other goods or services this sort of barter exchange is rarely seen.

Quality	Quality in business, engineering and manufacturing has a pragmatic interpretation as the non-inferiority or superiority of something. Quality is a perceptual, conditional and somewhat subjective attribute and may be understood differently by different people. Consumers may focus on the specification quality of a product/service, or how it compares to competitors in the marketplace.
Portfolio	In finance, a portfolio is a collection of investments held by an institution or an individual. Holding a portfolio is a part of an investment and risk-limiting strategy called diversification. By owning several assets, certain types of risk (in particular specific risk) can be reduced.
Electric	The Electric VLSI Design System is an EDA tool written by Steven M. Rubin. Electric is used to draw schematics and to do integrated circuit layout. It can also handle hardware description languages such as VHDL and Verilog.
Game theory	Game theory is a branch of applied mathematics that is used in the social sciences, most notably in economics, as well as in biology (particularly evolutionary biology and ecology), engineering, political science, international relations, computer science, social psychology, philosophy and management. Game theory attempts to mathematically capture behavior in strategic situations, or games, in which an individual's success in making choices depends on the choices of others (Myerson, 1991). While initially developed to analyze competitions in which one individual does better at another's expense (zero sum games), it has been expanded to treat a wide class of interactions, which are classified according to several criteria.
Transaction	In data mining, a transaction is an element of a family of a set of items. In other words, the transaction is a subset of the set of items.

Chapter 2. DESIGNING STRATEGY

Let I be a set of items and $\mathcal{T}$ be a family of sets over I.

Transaction cost	In economics and related disciplines, a transaction cost is a cost incurred in making an economic exchange (restated: the cost of participating in a market). For example, most people, when buying or selling a stock, must pay a commission to their broker; that commission is a transaction cost of doing the stock deal. Or consider buying a banana from a store; to purchase the banana, your costs will be not only the price of the banana itself, but also the energy and effort it requires to find out which of the various banana products you prefer, where to get them and at what price, the cost of traveling from your house to the store and back, the time waiting in line, and the effort of the paying itself; the costs above and beyond the cost of the banana are the transaction costs.
Corporate sustainability	Corporate sustainability is a business approach that creates long-term consumer and employee value by not only creating a "green" strategy aimed towards the natural environment, but taking into consideration every dimension of how a business operates in the social, cultural, and economic environment. Also formulating strategies to build a company that fosters longevity through transparency and proper employee development.

Corporate sustainability is an evolution on more traditional phrases describing ethical corporate practice. |
| Lean manufacturing | Lean manufacturing, often simply, "Lean," is a production practice that considers the expenditure of resources for any goal other than the creation of value for the end customer to be wasteful, and thus a target for elimination. Working from the perspective of the customer who consumes a product or service, "value" is defined as any action or process that a customer would be willing to pay for. Basically, lean is centered on preserving value with less work. |
| Negotiation | Negotiation is a dialogue between two or more people or parties, intended to reach an understanding, resolve point of difference, or gain advantage in outcome of dialogue, to produce an agreement upon courses of action, to bargain for individual or collective advantage, to craft outcomes to satisfy various interests of two person/ parties involved in negotiation process. Negotiation is a process where each party involved in negotiating tries to gain an advantage for themselves by the end of the process. Negotiation is intended to aim at compromise. |

CTAM101

Chapter 2. DESIGNING STRATEGY

Global strategy	Global strategy as defined in business terms is an organization's strategic guide to globalization. A sound global strategy should address these questions: what must be (versus what is) the extent of market presence in the world's major markets? How to build the necessary global presence? What must be (versus what is) the optimal locations around the world for the various value chain activities? How to run global presence into global competitive advantage? Academic research on global strategy came of age during the 1980s, including work by Michael Porter and Christopher Bartlett ' Sumantra Ghoshal. Among the forces perceived to bring about the globalization of competition were convergence in economic systems and technological change, especially in information technology, that facilitated and required the coordination of a multinational firm's strategy on a worldwide scale.
Globalization	Globalization describes the process by which regional economies, societies, and cultures have become integrated through a global network of political ideas through communication, transportation, and trade. The term is most closely associated with the term economic globalization: the integration of national economies into the international economy through trade, foreign direct investment, capital flows, migration, the spread of technology, and military presence. However, globalization is usually recognized as being driven by a combination of economic, technological, sociocultural, political, and biological factors.
Strategie	The monthly title Strategie - Pismo Dyrektorów Finansowych is Polands only magazine for corporate financial managers. With a printrun of 10 200 the business-to-business-title is distributed in subscription and controlled circulation through the major Polish press distributors RUCH, Kolporter, Garmond and GLM. Editorial partners The editorial team of Strategie co-operates with industry- and consultancy-specialists. Contributors include representatives of the Polish Employers Association Lewiatan (Rada Podatkowa), PCTA Polish Corporate Treasurers Association, Warsaw School of Economics, Warsaw University of Technology, Deloitte, KPMG, PricewaterhouseCoopers and Capgemini.

Chapter 2. DESIGNING STRATEGY

Nike	In Greek mythology, Nike was a goddess who personified victory, also known as the Winged Goddess of Victory. The Roman equivalent was Victoria. Depending upon the time of various myths, she was described as the daughter of Pallas (Titan) and Styx (Water), and the sister of Kratos (Strength), Bia (Force), and Zelus (Zeal).
Decline	Decline is a change over time from previously efficient to inefficient organizational functioning, from previously rational to non-rational organizational and individual decision-making, from previously law-abiding to law violating organizational and individual behavior, from previously virtuous to iniquitous individual moral behavior. Note: The word decline should not be confused with the word obsolete. Decline refers to the degenerating of something whereas obsolete refers to the outdating of something or that it is no longer in use.Is the prosses of declining,a gradual sinking and wasting away.
Turnaround	A turnaround is an arrangement in the film industry, whereby the rights to a project one studio has developed are sold to another studio in exchange for the cost of development plus interest.
	Michael Cieply defined the term in The New York Times as "arrangements under which producers can move a project from one studio to another under certain conditions".
	The turnaround of The Boondock Saints is documented in Overnight, a 2003 documentary which mainly focuses on the perspective of how director Troy Duffy "fell" in Hollywood.
Bankruptcy	Bankruptcy is a legal status of a person or a organisation that cannot repay the debts it owes to its creditors. Creditors may file a bankruptcy petition against a business or corporate debtor ("involuntary bankruptcy") in an effort to recoup a portion of what they are owed or initiate a restructuring. In the majority of cases, however, bankruptcy is initiated by the debtor (a "voluntary bankruptcy" that is filed by the insolvent individual or organization).
Corporation	A corporation is a legal entity that is created under the laws of a State designed to establish the entity as a separate legal entity having its own privileges and liabilities distinct from those of its members. There are many different forms of corporations, most of which are used to conduct business. Early corporations were established by charter and many of these chartered companies still exist.

CRam101

Energy	Mental or psychic energy is the concept of a principle of activity powering the operation of the mind or psyche. Many modern psychologists or neuroscientists would equate it with increased metabolism in neurons of the brain. Philosophical accounts The idea harks back to Aristotle's conception of actus et potentia.
Scenario	In computing, a scenario is a narrative describing foreseeable interactions of types of users (characters) and the system. Scenarios include information about goals, expectations, motivations, actions and reactions. Scenarios are neither predictions nor forecasts, but rather attempts to reflect on or portray the way in which a system is used in the context of daily activity.
Scenario planning	Scenario planning, is a strategic planning method that some organizations use to make flexible long-term plans. It is in large part an adaptation and generalization of classic methods used by military intelligence. The original method was that a group of analysts would generate simulation games for policy makers.

Chapter 3. IMPLEMENTING STRATEGY

Strategy	Strategy, a word of military origin, refers to a plan of action designed to achieve a particular goal. In military usage strategy is distinct from tactics, which are concerned with the conduct of an engagement, while strategy is concerned with how different engagements are linked. How a battle is fought is a matter of tactics: the terms and conditions that it is fought on and whether it should be fought at all is a matter of strategy, which is part of the four levels of warfare: political goals or grand strategy, strategy, operations, and tactics.
Core	A core is a device used in casting and molding processes to produce internal cavities and reentrant angles. The core is normally a disposable item that is destroyed to get it out of the piece. They are most commonly used in sand casting, but are also used in injection molding.
Perspective	Perspective in the graphic arts, such as drawing, is an approximate representation, on a flat surface (such as paper), of an image as it is seen by the eye. The two most characteristic features of perspective are that objects are drawn: • Smaller as their distance from the observer increases • Foreshortened: the size of an object's dimensions along the line of sight are relatively shorter than dimensions across the line of sight Overview Linear perspective works by representing the light that passes from a scene through an imaginary rectangle (the painting), to the viewer's eye. It is similar to a viewer looking through a window and painting what is seen directly onto the windowpane.
Strategie	The monthly title Strategie - Pismo Dyrektorów Finansowych is Polands only magazine for corporate financial managers. With a printrun of 10 200 the business-to-business-title is distributed in subscription and controlled circulation through the major Polish press distributors RUCH, Kolporter, Garmond and GLM. Editorial partners

Chapter 3. IMPLEMENTING STRATEGY

The editorial team of Strategie co-operates with industry- and consultancy-specialists. Contributors include representatives of the Polish Employers Association Lewiatan (Rada Podatkowa), PCTA Polish Corporate Treasurers Association, Warsaw School of Economics, Warsaw University of Technology, Deloitte, KPMG, PricewaterhouseCoopers and Capgemini.

Corporate sustainability

Corporate sustainability is a business approach that creates long-term consumer and employee value by not only creating a "green" strategy aimed towards the natural environment, but taking into consideration every dimension of how a business operates in the social, cultural, and economic environment. Also formulating strategies to build a company that fosters longevity through transparency and proper employee development.

Corporate sustainability is an evolution on more traditional phrases describing ethical corporate practice.

Chief executive

Chief Executive is a term used for certain gubernatorial offices, expressing the nature of their job being analogous to a head of government. Commonly used to refer to Presidential powers given by the constitution. As Chief Executive the president can: implement policy, supervise executive branch of government, prepare executive budget for submission to congress, and appoint and remove executive officials

While in most cases there is another specific style, such as (lieutenant-)governor(-general), there are a few offices formally styled Chief Executive:

- in the People's Republic of China, in two special administrative regions that were under foreign colonial rule until their recent transfer of sovereignty, where the chief executive are heads of the regions and heads of government:

- in Mauritius, on Rodrigues island, since 12 October 2002 autonomy was granted:

- New Zealand Antarctic Territory: while not a government, the Ross Dependency is a Crown entity managed by a Board of Directors and the Chair acts as the Chief Executive.

Chapter 3. IMPLEMENTING STRATEGY

Chief executive officer	A chief executive officer, managing director, or chief executive is the highest-ranking corporate officer (executive) or administrator in charge of total management of an organization. An individual appointed as a Chief executive officer of a corporation, company, organization, or agency reports to the board of directors. Many Chief executive officers have the title "president and Chief executive officer".
Organizational structure	An organizational structure consists of activities such as task allocation, coordination and supervision, which are directed towards the achievement of organizational aims. It can also be considered as the viewing glass or perspective through which individuals see their organization and its environment. Many organizations have hierarchical structures, but not all.
Board of directors	A board of directors is a body of elected or appointed members who jointly oversee the activities of a company or organization. The body sometimes has a different name, such as board of trustees, board of governors, board of managers, or executive board. It is often simply referred to as "the board." A board's activities are determined by the powers, duties, and responsibilities delegated to it or conferred on it by an authority outside itself.
Director	Director refers to a rank in management. A director is a person who leads, or supervises a certain area of a company, a program, or a project. Usually companies, which use this title commonly have large numbers of people with the title of director with different categories (e.g. director of human resources).
Matrix	In hot metal typesetting, a matrix is a mold for casting the letters known as sorts used in letterpress printing.

Clam101

Chapter 3. IMPLEMENTING STRATEGY

	In letterpress typography the matrix of one letter is inserted into the bottom of a hand mould, the mould is locked and molten type metal is poured into a straight-sided vertical cavity above the matrix. When the metal has cooled and solidified the mould is unlocked and a newly-cast metal sort is removed, ready for composition with other sorts.
Strategic business unit	Strategic Business Unit is understood as a business unit within the overall corporate identity which is distinguishable from other business because it serves a defined external market where management can conduct strategic planning in relation to products and markets. The unique small business unit benefits that a firm aggressively promotes in a consistent manner. When companies become really large, they are best thought of as being composed of a number of businesses (or Strategic business units).
Team	TEAM, formerly known as Team of Destiny, is a leadership development company founded by Orrin Woodward and Chris Brady in 1999 in Michigan. TEAM is an acronym that stands for TEAM. Woodward and Brady are former IBOs (Independent Business Owners, a.k.a. distributors) of the multi-level marketing company Quixtar, as well as members of the board of directors of Quixtar's IBOAI (IBO Association International, representing Quixtar IBOs).
Mission statement	A mission statement is a formal, short, written statement of the purpose of a company or organization. The mission statement should guide the actions of the organization, spell out its overall goal, provide a sense of direction, and guide decision-making. It provides "the framework or context within which the company's strategies are formulated." Historically it is associated with Christian religious groups; indeed, for many years, a missionary was assumed to be a person on a specifically religious mission.
PeopleSoft	PeopleSoft, Inc. was a company that provided human resource management systems (HRMS) and customer relationship management (CRM) software, as well as software solutions for manufacturing, financials, enterprise performance management, and student administration to large corporations, governments, and organizations. It existed as an independent corporation until its acquisition by Oracle Corporation in 2005. The PeopleSoft name and product line are now marketed by Oracle.

Chapter 3. IMPLEMENTING STRATEGY

Corporate social responsibility	Corporate social responsibility is a form of corporate self-regulation integrated into a business model. Corporate social responsibility policy functions as a built-in, self-regulating mechanism whereby business monitors and ensures its active compliance with the spirit of the law, ethical standards, and international norms. The goal of Corporate social responsibility is to embrace responsibility for the company's actions and encourage a positive impact through its activities on the environment, consumers, employees, communities, stakeholders and all other members of the public sphere.
Stakeholder	A corporate stakeholder is a party that can affect or be affected by the actions of the business as a whole. The stakeholder concept was first used in a 1963 internal memorandum at the Stanford Research institute. It defined stakeholders as "those groups without whose support the organization would cease to exist." The theory was later developed and championed by R. Edward Freeman in the 1980s.
Stakeholder theory	The stakeholder theory is a theory of organizational management and business ethics that addresses morals and values in managing an organization. It was originally detailed by R. Edward Freeman in the book Strategic Management: A Stakeholder Approach, and identifies and models the groups which are stakeholders of a corporation, and both describes and recommends methods by which management can give due regard to the interests of those groups. In short, it attempts to address the "Principle of Who or What Really Counts." Overview In the traditional view of the firm, the shareholder view (the only one recognized in business law in most countries), the shareholders or stockholders are the owners of the company, and the firm has a binding fiduciary duty to put their needs first, to increase value for them.
Strategic management	Strategic management is a field that deals with the major intended and emergent initiatives taken by general managers on behalf of owners, involving utilization of resources, to enhance the performance of ?rms in their external environments. It entails specifying the organization's mission, vision and objectives, developing policies and plans, often in terms of projects and programs, which are designed to achieve these objectives, and then allocating resources to implement the policies and plans, projects and programs. A balanced scorecard is often used to evaluate the overall performance of the business and its progress towards objectives. Recent studies and leading management theorists have advocated that strategy needs to start with stakeholders expectations and use a modified balanced scorecard which includes all stakeholders.

Chapter 3. IMPLEMENTING STRATEGY

Compact	A compact is cosmetic product. It is usually contained in a small, round case, with two or all of the following: a mirror, pressed powder, and a powder puff. The term is an abbreviation for "compact powder".
John Smedley	John Smedley is the name of four generations of owners of Lea Mills, near Matlock, Derbyshire. The most famous of these was John Smedley born Wirksworth, Derbyshire. Lea Mills Lea Mills was founded in 1784 by Peter Nightingale (an ancestor of Florence Nightingale) (former accountant to Richard Arkwright), and John Smedley.
John Deere	Deere ' Company, usually known by its brand name John Deere is an American corporation based in Moline, Illinois, and the leading manufacturer of agricultural machinery in the world. In 2008, it was listed as 102nd in the Fortune 500 ranking. Deere and Company agricultural products, usually sold under the John Deere name, include tractors, combine harvesters, balers, planters/seeders, ATVs and forestry equipment.
Balanced scorecard	The balanced scorecard is a strategic performance management tool - a semi-standard structured report supported by proven design methods and automation tools that can be used by managers to keep track of the execution of activities by staff within their control and monitor the consequences arising from these actions. It is perhaps the best known of several such frameworks . Since 2000, use of Balanced Scorecard, its derivatives (e.g. performance prism), and other similar tools (e.g. Results Based Management) have become common in the Middle East, Asia and Spanish-speaking countries also.
Business process	A business process is a collection of related, structured activities or tasks that produce a specific service or product (serve a particular goal) for a particular customer or customers. It often can be visualized with a flowchart as a sequence of activities. Overview

Chapter 3. IMPLEMENTING STRATEGY

There are three types of business processes:

1. Management processes, the processes that govern the operation of a system.

Customer

A customer is usually used to refer to a current or potential buyer or user of the products of an individual or organization, called the supplier, seller, or vendor. This is typically through purchasing or renting goods or services. However, in certain contexts, the term customer also includes by extension any entity that uses or experiences the services of another.

Hotel

A hotel is an establishment that provides paid lodging on a short-term basis. The provision of basic accommodation, in times past, consisting only of a room with a bed, a cupboard, a small table and a washstand has largely been replaced by rooms with modern facilities, including en-suite bathrooms and air conditioning or climate control. Additional common features found in hotel rooms are a telephone, an alarm clock, a television, a safe, a mini-bar with snack foods and drinks, and facilities for making tea and coffee.

Chapter 4. INDUSTRY ANALYIS

Lodging	Lodging is a type of residential accommodation. People who travel and stay away from home for more than a day need lodging for sleep, rest, safety, shelter from cold temperatures or rain, storage of luggage and access to common household functions. Lodgings may be self catering in which case no food is laid on but cooking facilities are available.
Hotel	A hotel is an establishment that provides paid lodging on a short-term basis. The provision of basic accommodation, in times past, consisting only of a room with a bed, a cupboard, a small table and a washstand has largely been replaced by rooms with modern facilities, including en-suite bathrooms and air conditioning or climate control. Additional common features found in hotel rooms are a telephone, an alarm clock, a television, a safe, a mini-bar with snack foods and drinks, and facilities for making tea and coffee.
Rate	In mathematics, a rate is a ratio between two measurements, often with different units.. If the unit or quantity in respect of which something is changing is not specified, usually the rate is per unit time. However, a rate of change can be specified per unit time, or per unit of length or mass or another quantity.
Rates	Rates are a type of taxation system in the United Kingdom, and in places with systems deriving from the British one, the proceeds of which are used to fund local government. Some other countries have taxes with a more or less comparable role, for example France's taxe d'habitation. Rates by country Hong Kong In Hong Kong, rates on property is based on the nominal rental value of the property.

Chapter 4. INDUSTRY ANALYIS

Corporation	A corporation is a legal entity that is created under the laws of a State designed to establish the entity as a separate legal entity having its own privileges and liabilities distinct from those of its members. There are many different forms of corporations, most of which are used to conduct business. Early corporations were established by charter and many of these chartered companies still exist.
Group	In mathematics, a group is an algebraic structure consisting of a set together with an operation that combines any two of its elements to form a third element. To qualify as a group, the set and the operation must satisfy a few conditions called group axioms, namely closure, associativity, identity and invertibility. Many familiar mathematical structures such as number systems obey these axioms: for example, the integers endowed with the addition operation form a group.
Market	• A market is any one of a variety of systems, institutions, procedures, social relations and infrastructures whereby parties engage in exchange. While parties may exchange goods and services by barter, most markets rely on buyers offer their goods or services (including labor) in exchange for money (legal tender such as fiat money) from buyers. For a market to be competitive, there must be more than a single buyer or seller.
Market segmentation	Market segmentation is a concept in economics and marketing. A market segment is a sub-set of a market made up of people or organizations with one or more characteristics that cause them to demand similar product and/or services based on qualities of those products such as price or function. A true market segment meets all of the following criteria: it is distinct from other segments (different segments have different needs), it is homogeneous within the segment (exhibits common needs); it responds similarly to a market stimulus, and it can be reached by a market intervention.
Financial analysis	Financial analysis refers to an assessment of the viability, stability and profitability of a business, sub-business or project.

It is performed by professionals who prepare reports using ratios that make use of information taken from financial statements and other reports. These reports are usually presented to top management as one of their bases in making business decision.

Leverage

In statistics, leverage is a term used in connection with regression analysis and, in particular, in analyses aimed at identifying those observations which have a large effect on the outcome of fitting regression models.

Leverage points are those observations, if any, made at extreme or outlying values of the independent variables such that the lack of neighbouring observations means that the fitted regression model will pass close to that particular observation.

Modern computer packages for statistical analysis include, as part of their facilities for regression analysis, various quantitative measures for identifying influential observations: among these measures is partial leverage, a measure of how a variable contributes to the leverage of a datum.

Profit

In accounting, profit can be considered to be the difference between the purchase price and the costs of bringing to market whatever it is that is accounted as an enterprise (whether by harvest, extraction, manufacture, or purchase) in terms of the component costs of delivered goods and/or services and any operating or other expenses.

There are several important profit measures in common use which will be explained in the following. Note that the words earnings, profit and income are used as substitutes in some of these terms (also depending on US vs. UK usage), thus inflating the number of profit measures.

Chapter 4. INDUSTRY ANALYIS

Ratio	In mathematics, a ratio is a relationship between two numbers of the same kind (i.e., objects, persons, students, spoonfuls, units of whatever identical dimension), usually expressed as "a to b" or a:b, sometimes expressed arithmetically as a dimensionless quotient of the two, which explicitly indicates how many times the first number contains the second. Notation and terminology The ratio of numbers A and B can be expressed as: • the ratio of A to B • A is to B • A:B The numbers A and B are sometimes called terms with A being the antecedent and B being the consequent. The proportion expressing the equality of the ratios A:B and C:D is written A:B=C:D or A:B::C:D. this latter form, when spoken or written in the English language, is often expressed as A is to B as C is to D. Again, A, B, C, D are called the terms of the proportion.
Mercury	Mercury (/ˈmɜːrkjəri/ or /ˈmɜːrkəri/ MER-k(y)ə-ree), also known as quicksilver or hydrargyrum, is a chemical element with the symbol Hg and atomic number 80. Mercury is the only metal that is liquid at standard conditions for temperature and pressure; the only other element that is liquid under these conditions is bromine. With a freezing point of −38.83 °C and boiling point of 356.73 °C, mercury has one of the broadest ranges of its liquid state of any metal. A heavy, silvery d-block metal, mercury is also one of the five metallic chemical elements that are liquid at or near room temperature and pressure, the others being caesium, francium, gallium, and rubidium.

Chapter 4. INDUSTRY ANALYIS

Case	A case of some merchandise is a collection of items packaged together. In the United States, typically a standard case contains a certain number of items depending on what the merchandise is. For consumer foodstuffs such as canned goods, soda, cereal and such, a case is typically 24 items, however cases may range from 12 to 36, typically in multiples of six.
Exchange	An exchange is a highly organized market where (especially) tradable securities, commodities, foreign exchange, futures, and options contracts are sold and bought.

Description

Exchanges bring together brokers and dealers who buy and sell these objects. These various financial instruments can typically be sold either through the exchange, typically with the benefit of a clearinghouse to cover defaults, or over-the-counter (OTC), where there is typically less protection against counterparty risk from clearinghouses although OTC clearinghouses have become more common over the years, with regulators placing pressure on the OTC markets to clear and display trades openly.

Exchanges can be subdivided:

- by objects sold:
    - stock exchange or securities exchange
    - commodities exchange
    - foreign exchange market - is rare today in the form of a specialized institution
- by type of trade:
    - classical exchange - for spot trades
    - futures exchange or futures and options exchange - for derivatives

In practise, futures exchanges are usually commodity exchanges, i.e. all derivatives, including financial derivatives, are usually traded at commodity exchanges.

Chapter 4. INDUSTRY ANALYIS

Fair Trade	Fair trade is an organized social movement and market-based approach that aims to help producers in developing countries make better trading conditions and promote sustainability. The movement advocates the payment of a higher price to producers as well as higher social and environmental standards. It focuses in particular on exports from developing countries to developed countries, most notably handicrafts, coffee, cocoa, sugar, tea, bananas, honey, cotton, wine, fresh fruit, chocolate, flowers and gold.
Fair Trade Coffee	Fair trade coffee is coffee which is purchased directly from the growers for a higher price than standard coffee. Fair trade coffee is one of many fair trade certified products available around the world. The purpose of fair trade is to promote healthier working conditions and greater economic incentive for producers.
Retailing	Retail consists of the sale of goods or merchandise from a fixed location, such as a department store, boutique or kiosk, or by mail, in small or individual lots for direct consumption by the purchaser. Retailing may include subordinated services, such as delivery. Purchasers may be individuals or businesses.

Chapter 5. SEMESTER PROJECTS

Team

TEAM, formerly known as Team of Destiny, is a leadership development company founded by Orrin Woodward and Chris Brady in 1999 in Michigan. TEAM is an acronym that stands for TEAM.

Woodward and Brady are former IBOs (Independent Business Owners, a.k.a. distributors) of the multi-level marketing company Quixtar, as well as members of the board of directors of Quixtar's IBOAI (IBO Association International, representing Quixtar IBOs).

MICA

The mica group of sheet silicate (phyllosilicate) minerals includes several closely related materials having highly perfect basal cleavage. All are monoclinic with a tendency towards pseudo-hexagonal crystals and are similar in chemical composition. The highly perfect cleavage, which is the most prominent characteristic of mica, is explained by the hexagonal sheet-like arrangement of its atoms.

Cram101

Lightning Source UK Ltd.
Milton Keynes UK
UKHW030651110419

340868UK00003B/542/P